ALLIGATORS &
CROCODILES

ERIK D. STOOPS &
DEBBIE LYNNE STONE

 Sterling Publishing Co., Inc., New York

This book is lovingly dedicated to Ken and Sharon Earnest of South Dakota, whose dedication to the preservation of the many crocodilian species will enable future generations to see and learn about these fascinating reptiles.

Library of Congress Cataloging-in-Publication Data

Stoops, Erik D.
    Alligators & crocodiles / Erik D. Stoops & Debbie Lynne Stone.
      p.   cm.
    Includes index.
    ISBN 0-8069-0422-4
    1. Alligators—Miscellanea—Juvenile literature. 2. Crocodiles—
Miscellanea—Juvenile literature. [1. Alligators—Miscellanea.
2. Crocodiles—Miscellanea. 3. Questions and answers.] I. Stone,
Debbie Lynne. II. Title. III. Title: Alligators and crocodiles.
QL666.C925S79 1994
597.98—dc20
                                          94–15691
                                             CIP
                                             AC

Cover photo: American Alligator, by Larry Lipsky/Tom Stack & Associates

Design by Judy Morgan

1 3 5 7 9 10 8 6 5 4 2

Published by Sterling Publishing Company, Inc.
387 Park Avenue South, New York, N.Y. 10016
© 1994 by Erik D. Stoops and Debbie Lynne Stone
Distributed in Canada by Sterling Publishing
% Canadian Manda Group, P.O. Box 920, Station U
Toronto, Ontario, Canada M8Z 5P9
Distributed in Great Britain and Europe by Cassell PLC
Villiers House, 41/47 Strand, London WC2N 5JE, England
Distributed in Australia by Capricorn Link (Australia) Pty Ltd.
P.O. Box 6651, Baulkham Hills, Business Centre, NSW 2153, Australia
Printed and bound in China
Sterling ISBN 0-8069-0422-4

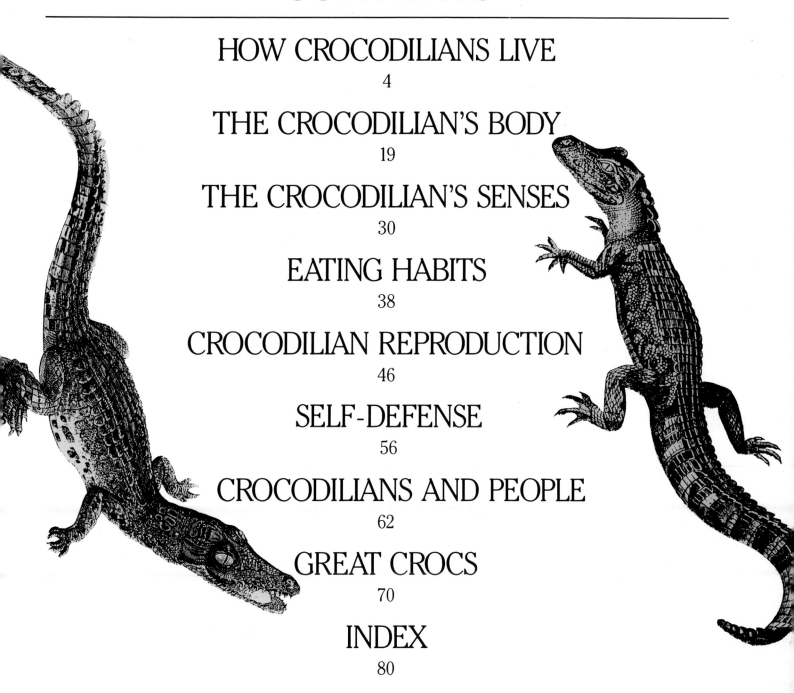

CONTENTS

HOW CROCODILIANS LIVE

◄ The American Alligator got its name from the Spanish word, "el lagarto," which means lizard.

▼ Ancestors of the Nile Crocodile may have existed during the Age of the Dinosaurs.

Crocodilians are some of the closest living relatives of the dinosaurs. What are the differences between the species? Where do they live? How fast do they swim? These questions are asked often. Here are some of the answers.

By Sharon Earnest

What are crocodilians?

By Terry Christopher

Crocodilians (crock-uh-*dill*-yuns) are the group of reptiles that includes alligators, crocodiles, caimans and gharials. Their outer bodies are like lizards', with scales and hard plates that make them look as if they're wearing armor.

All crocodilians have long snouts, long muscular tails, four short legs and tough teeth.

5

What is a "plate" and what's it made of?

The plates are thick, tough, bony parts of the skin that help protect the crocodilian. These plates also act as solar panels to collect heat and warm the animal. Some crocodilians have a lot of plates; others don't. The more plates a croc has, the less flexible it is in its movements.

▼ The American Alligator's bony back plates join the thick scales of its neck, making it look as if it's wearing armor.

By National Park Service. Patricia Caulfield

What's the difference between a crocodile and an alligator?

Actually, there are very few physical differences. Crocodiles are longer and heavier than alligators, and they also have a worse temper. Generally, they have narrower jaws and a longer pointed snout. Plus, there are more crocodile species than alligator.

By Sharon Earnest

◄ This is the skull of an alligator. You can see that it is much shorter in the snout than the crocodile skull.

► This is the skull of a crocodile. If you look closely, you can see that the crocodile has many more teeth than the alligator, and it is longer in the snout.

By Sharon Earnest

How can you tell crocodiles and alligators apart?

Some people think you can tell them apart by the shape of their snout. This is not always true. One way to tell the difference is by looking at their teeth. When a crocodile's mouth is closed, you can see a large bottom tooth sticking up. An alligator's teeth don't show when its mouth is closed.

▲ The gharial's sharp teeth overlap when its mouth is closed.

▼ This Nile Crocodile's bottom teeth show when its mouth is closed.

7

What are gharials?

Gharials (gare-ee-als) are the most distinctive-looking of all crocodilian species. They have a long, narrow snout and light olive or tan skin. Male gharials have a nostril that can be closed and inflated so that it looks like a little balloon. Gharials can grow to almost 15 feet (4.5 m) long! Gavial (gay-vee-al) is another name for the same species. (Experts call them gharials.)

▲ The gharial has the longest snout of any crocodilian. It also has more teeth.

What are caimans?

There are three different species of caimans (kay-muns) in the crocodilian family: Caiman, Dwarf Caiman and Black Caiman. Most caimans do not grow more than eight feet (2.4 m) long. But one species, the Black Caiman, can grow bigger than the caiman's closest relative, the alligator.

◄ Caimans look a lot like alligators because their lower teeth don't show when their mouths are closed. This Spectacled Caiman is a good example.

Are crocodilians cold-blooded?

Yes. The croc's temperature depends on outside temperatures, so its heart can speed up or slow down as needed. This controls the flow of blood that cools or warms the animal.

▶ Crocodiles and alligators cool off by slipping into the water at night. By morning, they need to sun themselves again.

Do all crocodilians warm and cool themselves in the same way?

No, some species only surface for a short time in the morning, then stay underwater the rest of the day, and return to land at night.

How do crocodiles and alligators raise their temperature?

They warm themselves on the shore in the morning sun. In the afternoon, they float on top of the water. The sun on their backs helps their temperature to stay about the same all day.

By Terry Christopher

Do all crocodiles and alligators live in the tropics?

Most of them. Only two species—the American Alligator and the Chinese Alligator—can survive in colder temperatures. All other crocodilians must live in a warm climate to survive. If the temperature falls below 40°F (4.4°C), most crocs are in danger of dying.

▼ The Chinese Alligator is rarely seen in the wild today because its habitat has been destroyed.

By Sharon Earnest

▲ This baby American Alligator has just hatched and is getting ready to yawn. American Alligators live only in the southeastern part of the United States.

By Sharon Earnest

10

Where do alligators live?

They usually live in rivers, wetlands or swamps in many parts of the world.

▶ Alligators in the Florida Everglades blend in well with the scenery and can take visitors by surprise.

Where do crocodiles live?

Crocodiles live in freshwater rivers, lakes and ponds. Some species can live in salt water. They are found in many parts of Africa, southern Asia and northern Australia. Other species also inhabit Mexico, Central America, northern South America and the Caribbean islands.

▶ Gharials are so rare today that most of them can be seen only in zoos.

By Dr. James Dixon, Texas A&M University

Where do caimans and gharials live?

Caimans are found in the tropical areas of Mexico, Central and South America.

Gharials live in the rivers of northern India, Nepal, Pakistan and Bangladesh.

By Sharon Earnest

Can any crocodilians survive in ice and snow?

Some alligators can survive in freezing water, but that's only because it's warmer under the surface of the ice. As long as there is a break in the ice so that the alligator can breathe, it can manage to live in cold water for a long time. Crocodiles, caimans and gharials cannot survive in cold temperatures.

Do alligators hibernate?

No, but they don't move around much in the winter. They go into a sort of sleep in which their body temperature drops down below the level needed for their everyday activity. If the weather warms up during the winter, they will become more active. Alligators don't eat much during cold weather, relying on their stored fat to survive.

Do crocodiles hibernate?

During the dry season, when there isn't much rain, crocodiles may become sluggish, refuse to feed and bury themselves in the mud. Scientists call this a mild hibernation period.

▼ During cold weather, alligators stay in shallow water, with just their nostrils above the surface for breathing.

By Terry Christopher

By the Audubon Zoo

How many different kinds of crocodilians are there?

There are two types of alligators, 13 types of crocodiles, 7–8 kinds of caimans, one species of gharial—and then there is the False Gharial, from Borneo and Malaysia, that is in a family by itself. Its head looks like a gharial, its tail is big and powerful like a Saltwater Crocodile and its body looks like an alligator!

Are there albino alligators?

Yes, but they are rare. Albino alligators do not survive long in the wild because their colors don't blend in with their surroundings.

▲ **This baby white alligator is not a true albino, because its eyes are blue instead of pink.**

▼ **This American Alligator is resting in the sun. Although its eyes are closed, it is aware of its surroundings and is not asleep.**

How long do crocodilians sleep?

Scientists believe that crocodilians just catnap now and then. They usually stay awake and are aware of what's going on around them.

By Terry Christopher

How much do crocodilians weigh?

Anywhere from two ounces (a hatchling) to 2,000 pounds (908 kg). The largest known crocodile in the world was Biggy, a Saltwater Crocodile that lived in the National Zoo in Washington, D.C. When he died in 1974, he weighed almost a ton (.9 metric tons).

▶ **Many species, like this Chinese Alligator, gain weight during the summer and store the fat all over their bodies for the winter months. They look fat, but it's only temporary.**

By Terry Christopher

By Sharon Earnest

How long are crocs?

The length depends on the species. It can range from 4 to 20 feet (1.2m to 6m).

◀ **This rare Siamese Crocodile measures almost 12 feet (3.6m) long and may grow larger.**

14

What are croc homes like?

Crocs make dens in the banks of lakes, streams and marshes. The animals use their dens as a safe retreat.

▶ The American Alligator (shown here) and the Chinese Alligator live thousands of miles apart but are the only two species of alligator in the world. They are very similar, which suggests that they were actually just one species many years ago.

By National Park Service, Carl G. Degen, Jr.

By Sharon Earnest

▲ The False Gharial, like many species of crocodilian, looks for a sandy beach away from flood waters to make its nest.

How do crocodilians make their nests?

Some crocodiles nest by digging a hole in the sand. Some species make their nests by piling up grass, mud, leaves, twigs and branches. Usually they nest next to a stream. Alligators always make huge piled-up nests that may be as high as three feet (.9 m). They use their hind legs to shovel everything into a heap. Then they pack the nest down by crawling all over it.

15

Can crocodilians swim fast?

While crocs usually cruise slowly, they can swim very rapidly—sometimes as fast as 20 miles (32 km) per hour—when chasing prey. They can even leap out of the water and appear to "tail walk"!

How long can crocodilians stay underwater?

Crocodilians can hold their breath for more than an hour!

By Sharon Earnest

By R. Reed

▲ This Cuban Crocodile, like other crocs, will often dive into deep water to hunt for prey.

▲ This False Gharial is cruising underwater at a slow speed. False Gharials got their name

Do crocs ever go in deep water?

Yes, they often dive into deeper water or lie on the bottom of a river to escape danger.

because they look like Indian Gharials but have buckteeth instead of pointy straight ones.

How fast can crocs move on land?

When crocodilians are trying to catch prey, they can run as fast as 11 miles (17.6 km) per hour for short distances of about 100 yards (91 m). Crocodilians also do a "high walk" or a scuttle belly run on land, which is slower than their running or galloping.

By Sharon Earnest

▲ **This Broad-Nosed Caiman looks as if it is directly related to the dinosaurs.**

How long ago did the first crocodilians live?

We know that some crocodilians lived at the same time as the dinosaurs, over 200 million years ago. Scientists are still puzzled about how the crocodilians survived while the dinosaurs became extinct.

Do crocs get sick?

Yes. Besides bacterial diseases and viruses (just like humans), they get dental diseases that can cause them to lose their teeth. Also, crocs can get upset stomachs from fighting or from too much heat.

How long do crocodilians live?

All crocodilians can live a long time if their environments stay stable. There have been reports of crocs living up to 100 years. Most of them live about 50 to 75 years.

What do crocodilians die of?

Many crocs die of natural causes, like old age. Some die from diseases. Others, such as baby crocs, have many enemies—birds and snakes—that eat them. Adult crocs may be killed by poachers.

By R. Reed

▲ **Climate and habitat are important to the croc's well-being.**

THE CROCODILIAN'S BODY

◄ The adult Saltwater Crocodile has such a hard, scaly body that no enemy can harm it—except for humans.

How big is a crocodilian's snout?

Crocodile snouts are narrow and pointy. Alligators' and caimans' are wide and round. Gharials have very long, narrow snouts.

With their scaly skin, huge jaws and big tails, crocs look as if they belong back in the Age of the Dinosaurs. But the crocodilian of today is quite different from its ancestors. The first crocodiles had long legs, short snouts and lived mostly on land. As they evolved, their bodies became more streamlined.

▲ This croc is keeping its nostrils above the surface of the water. Its method of breathing is similar to the way people breathe when they swim and snorkel.

◄ This gharial's teeth are different from its cousins'. They are smaller and there are more of them.

How does a croc breathe?

As long as the tip of a crocodilian's snout is out of the water, it can breathe. Since its nostrils are at the front end of its snout, it can remain almost totally out of sight underwater and still breathe without difficulty. When a crocodilian dives, its breathing stops!

How many nostrils does a croc have?

Four. Two of them, used for breathing, are on top of its skin. The other two are inside its head, located near the brain. These are used for smelling things.

How big are crocodilians' teeth?

There are two kinds of teeth. In the front of the mouth are big canines with sharp, cutting edges for puncturing and gripping their prey. In the back of the mouth are short, blunt molars for crushing prey.

▲ You can see the nostrils on the tip of the snout of this Cuban Crocodile.

▲ Crocodilians' front teeth are pointed and jagged, which helps them hold on to their prey.

20

By Sharon Earnest

▲ Some of this Saltwater Crocodile's teeth are half an inch (1.25cm) long. That's about as large as crocs' teeth get.

How often do crocs lose their teeth?

Crocs' teeth last about two years before falling out. Teeth in front are replaced more frequently than back teeth. It's different for young crocs. The teeth in the back of their mouths generally fall out first.

Are all of a croc's teeth sharp?

No. Some are sharp and some are blunt, just like humans'. Crocodilians have some very sharp teeth, but they only use them to attack their prey. They never use them—or any other teeth—for chewing.

How many teeth do crocs have?

They have 28–32 teeth in their lower jaw and 30–40 teeth in their upper jaw. The actual number varies with the species.

▼ This West African Dwarf Crocodile uses its teeth to catch fish and other small prey.

By R. Reed

How many teeth do baby crocs have?

Babies are born with a full set of teeth. The American Alligator baby, for example, is born with 80 teeth. Croc babies are also born with a little short tooth, called an egg tooth, on the tip of their snout. The baby uses this tooth to break out of the egg. The egg tooth usually falls off a day or two after the baby is born.

▼ The Smooth-Fronted Dwarf Caiman has very fragile teeth when it is young. They often fall out, but they grow back.

▲ This American Crocodile has used its egg tooth to crack open its shell.

▲ Baby croc teeth are not as sharp as adult teeth. They are more like tiny needles.

By Terry Christopher

Why do crocs look as if they're smiling?

Crocs usually have their mouths wide open, which makes them look as if they're laughing. Crocs' jaws are set far back in their head. That may help them look like they're smiling.

▲ This New Guinea Crocodile seems to be smiling for the camera!

Do crocs have tongues?

Yes. They have a broad tongue that is attached to the bottom of their mouth. The tongue doesn't move, so it plays no part in catching prey.

Do crocs drink water?

Yes, like all reptiles, crocs need water to help digest their food and to keep their systems healthy.

By Dr. James Dixon, Texas A&M University

By Sharon Earnest

▲ This American Crocodile's tongue remains still while the animal maneuvers food down its throat.

◄ Like most reptiles, crocodilians do not have lips.

23

Do crocs get water in their mouths when they go underwater?

Yes. Since they don't have lips, their mouth leaks. But they have a special flap that keeps water from getting down their throat. Because of the flap, crocodilians can't drown, no matter how much water they get in their mouth.

What kind of skin do crocodilians have?

Crocs have strong, smooth, leathery skin. All crocodilians have scales on their skin that vary in shape and strength. Some parts of the croc's body have scales that are tough, bony plates with horns on them. Some of these are similar to the plates on the back of the heavily armored dinosaur, the stegosaurus.

By Sharon Earnest

▲ The scales on the crocodilian's belly are quite different from those on its back.

By Sharon Earnest

◄ This is a close-up view of the alligator's scaly back, which protects it from enemies and also from the sun.

What color are crocodilians?

Grown alligators are greyish black. Most crocodilians and caimans are brownish green. Gharials are generally lighter in color. Crocodilians are usually the same color as the water they swim in. They blend in so well that they're hard to spot.

Does a croc's skin change color as it grows?

As babies, most species are brightly colored or patterned. When the crocs grow older, these colors and patterns usually fade. Unlike most crocs, the Black Caiman sometimes keeps its bold markings throughout its life.

▲ The Saltwater Crocodile in Australia often swims from island to island in the ocean. The salt in the water sometimes sticks to the croc's skin, giving it an ivory appearance.

▼ This Black Caiman is young. When it grows up, it will be completely black.

Do crocs have knees?

Yes. The croc's front limbs are like human arms. Its back legs have bendable knees. Its hips, shoulders and elbows all work the same way as ours.

▶ Like all crocs, this Broad-nosed Caiman's hind legs and knees work like a human's knees.

By Sharon Earnest

Do crocs have hips?

Yes. Using its hips, the crocodilian can raise itself off the ground and walk, instead of dragging its belly like a lizard.

◀ The Orinoco Crocodile is one of the few species that maneuvers well on land. Its habitat is rocky, so it gets a lot of practice moving around.

By Sharon Earnest

26

How many toes do crocs have?

Crocodilians have five toes on their front feet and four toes on their hind feet. The toes are all partly webbed. On its front feet, only four toes develop. The fifth toe is a bone inside the croc's body that never fully forms.

▲ The webbing between the toes of this crocodilian helps it maneuver in the water.

By Sharon Earnest

▲ Crocodile toes are very flexible and help the animal move around on land by giving it better balance. They also cushion its feet when running, and help it swim better.

Do crocs have claws?

Yes. There are claws or nails on four of the toes on each foot. Crocodilians use these claws for digging and scratching, but not for tearing food.

Do crocs have scales on their feet?

Yes, the scales are mini-versions of the scales on the rest of the croc's body.

How long are a croc's legs?

The length of a croc's legs depends on the size of the reptile. But its front legs are always shorter than its back legs.

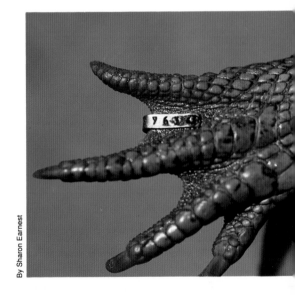

▲ Scientists often tag the legs of rare or endangered species for identification.

27

How do crocodilians get rid of body wastes?

Wastes are eliminated through the anal plate, an opening between the croc's back legs. It is protected by many outside scales. Inside the anal plate is the cloaca, which holds the reproductive organs.

How big is a croc's tail?

Tail size depends on the species, but the tail is usually equal in size to the rest of the body. As crocs grow older, they may lose bits of the end of their tail, which won't grow back.

▶ **The gharial uses its tail to help balance itself on land.**

By Sharon Earnest

28

By Sharon Earnest

Can crocs walk on their tails?

Sometimes crocs leap out of the water to catch a bird. When they perform this leap, they look as if they are "tail walking" like dolphins, but they really aren't.

▼ The gharial has long, scaly plates all the way down its tail, unlike other crocs. It uses this tail like a boat rudder to help it swim.

▲ The American Crocodile's tail is huge and can be a powerful weapon. The blow from an angry croc's tail can kill a large animal or a human.

What else does the croc's tail do?

It propels the croc through the water. With the help of its tail, some crocs can swim as fast as 20 miles (32 km) per hour!

By Sharon Earnest

29

THE CROCODILIAN'S SENSES

◄ **The Saltwater Crocodile's taste buds are accustomed to almost anything. This croc will eat whatever it is able to catch.**

C rocodilian senses are much more powerful than those of other reptiles in the world today. We know they have taste buds, because some of them prefer one type of food over another. Their eyes can focus on predators on land and in water practically at the same time. And they hear far better than most of their reptile cousins.

Do crocs have ears?

Crocs have two ears like we do. But their ears are found inside their head. All that shows on the outside are slits. When they dive, these slits are covered by a movable flap that protects their eardrums.

► **You can see the ear slits on the head of this Smooth-fronted Caiman.**

By R. Reed

Do crocs hear with their ears the way we do?

Yes. They can hear vibrations in the water and in the air just like people do.

Do crocodilians have good hearing?

They have great hearing. Their inner ear is very well developed and their hearing senses and nerves are right on top of their head. This super sense helps them find prey. They seem to be sensitive to a wide range of sounds. Their hearing is so good that they can hear their young calling from inside their eggshells!

▶ **This caiman's pupils have adjusted to the sunlight.**

How do a croc's eyes work?

Crocodilian eyes work like those of a cat. The pupils become small vertical slits when the croc is in the sun.

This blocks out the light like sunglasses. The pupil becomes large in the dark to allow more light to enter the eye.

Does a croc see clearly?

When its head is above water, its eyesight is very good. Underwater its vision is foggy, the way yours would be if you were looking through thick goggles.

By Sharon Earnest

◀ **This Nile Crocodile's pupils are small since it's daytime.**

By Sharon Earnest

What color are a croc's eyes?

That depends on the species. They are usually light yellow, light blue or light green. Some alligator species have black eyes.

By Terry Christopher

By R. Reed

▲ This American Alligator's eyes are dark blue, which is very rare. It is a genetic mutation.

◄ Like many other caimans, this Smooth-fronted Caiman's eyes are reddish brown.

► Most gharials have green eyes. They gleam white at night.

By Sharon Earnest

How do crocs see at night?

Crocs have vertical pupils in their eyes that open wide at night to allow more light to enter than a round pupil could. There is also a layer in the crocs' eyes that reflects light. At sunrise, or when you flash a light on a group of crocs at night, their eyes gleam like fireflies or dancing balls of light. It's very beautiful.

By R. Reed

Do crocs have eyelids?

Yes, they actually have three. Two of them are normal eyelids, like people's. The third eyelid is a transparent "flap" that slips over the eye. This third eyelid protects the reptile's eyes when it is underwater.

▲ These Nile Crocodiles use their keen eyesight, which is comparable to an owl's, to hunt prey above water.

▼ This white alligator will use its transparent third eyelid, like a pair of goggles, to see underwater.

Can crocs see colors?

Crocodilians seem to be able to tell the difference between some colors, such as red and yellow. Their retina (the screen at the back of their eyes) contains rods and cones, which give the animal color vision.

By Audubon Zoo

Do crocs feel pain?

We know that crocs feel pain because they sometimes flinch. If it is too hot on the ground where the crocodilian is standing, the animal will raise one paw at a time as if its feet were burning.

Do crocodiles cry?

No. Legend has it that crocodiles cry when they eat a person. Not true. Now it's said that people cry "crocodile tears" if they say they're sorry for something, but really aren't. Crocs do sometimes get watery eyes after they eat too large a piece of prey, but that isn't crying!

Can crocs smell things well?

Yes. Because of that second set of nostrils inside their heads, their sense of smell is very keen.

By Sharon Earnest

▲ **This rare baby African Dwarf Crocodile is able to use all its senses, including an excellent sense of smell, as soon as it is born.**

How do crocs communicate?

Crocodilians make many different sounds. They roar like thunder, grunt, growl, bellow, hiss and make sounds that are out of the range of human hearing. Crocs also communicate with loud head slaps in the water.

By Sharon Earnest

▲ **This baby Saltwater Crocodile is calling for its mother—by making sounds like a dog barking—while still in the egg!**

Do crocs usually hang out together?

Yes, crocs gather in the same general area. In many species crocs form groups made up of one male and four or five females.

▼ **Young crocs, such as these baby Cuban Crocodiles, often hang out together for the first few months of life.**

By R. Reed

By Dave Watts, Tom Stack & Assoc.

Do crocs have feelings for each other?

Crocs seem to care about each other. If a baby is calling in distress, all the crocs in the area will come to its aid. Crocs seem to be good parents and keep their babies close by.

Do crocs roam in "packs"?

No, they don't roam. They just stay together in places that are convenient for eating and resting.

▲ Many crocodilians, such as these gharials, like to rest in the sun and spend time with each other.

▶ These American Alligators have gathered in the same area because it's convenient for hunting prey.

By National Park Service. M. Woodbridge Williams

EATING HABITS

◀ The false gharial, like its cousin, the true gharial (shown on this page), only eats fish. That is all it is able to catch.

What do crocodilians eat?

Crocodilians eat mostly fish. But these animals, with their snapping jaws and speed, will catch and eat anything that wanders near the shore. They eat birds, turtles, frogs, and large animals like raccoons, sheep, dogs—even cows! Crocodilians have also been known to eat pigs, deer, horses, buffaloes, monkeys and elephants! Crocodilians will even eat dead animals, but only if the animal hasn't been dead very long.

▶ The gharials' jaws move with lightning-fast speed.

Crocodilians would be great in a speed-eating contest. Since they swallow their food whole, they never have to chew! Believe it or not, these ferocious reptiles seem quite polite when they eat. If several crocs are feeding on a large prey, such as a zebra, they take turns tearing off the chunks of flesh. Then they swim away to eat and get back on the end of the line to wait their turn for more to eat.

◀ Gharials' slender snouts and sharp teeth can easily snatch prey.

By Sharon Earnest

By Sharon Earnest

How do crocs eat?

Crocodilians rely a lot on gravity to help them eat. They juggle the food around in their jaws until they are comfortable with it in their mouth. Then, they toss back their head so the food falls down their throat.

Can a croc make its mouth bigger to swallow large prey?

No. Crocs only tear off chunks of flesh that they can swallow whole. They cannot dislocate their jaws to eat huge prey, the way some of the dinosaurs, such as Tyrannosaurus Rex, once did.

Do crocs ever eat other crocs?

It doesn't happen often, but sometimes adult crocs do attack weaker adult crocs. Some of the weaker adults may even attack and eat a younger croc or a baby.

By Sharon Earnest

By Sharon Earnest

◄ The gharial's teeth are all the same size, unlike other crocodilians. Its snout is very fragile and can break easily.

▼ The gharial sweeps its long snout in swift, sideways motions to capture its prey.

Do crocs taste their food?

Yes, crocs do seem to taste their food and can even tell the difference between sweet and sour.

40

By Sharon Earnest

▲ This baby Cuban Crocodile will feed on small fish and bugs until it is full.

How much do crocs eat at one time?

Generally, crocs eat until they are full. The quantity of food depends on the croc's size and species. Crocodilians can eat up to half their body weight at a time.

Do crocodilians eat together?

Sometimes if the prey is large, a group of crocs will share a meal.

▼ These young Cuban Crocodiles stay close to their mothers while eating small water insects and fish.

By Sharon Earnest

Do crocs ever throw up?

Yes, sometimes they get an upset stomach. Crocs may also throw up after being in a fight, getting too hot or when they're just not feeling well.

▶ Black Caimans, the largest species in the caiman family, sometimes feed on large animals.

By Sharon Earnest

41

How do crocs capture their prey?

The croc's powerful jaws clamp down on the animal. If the prey is caught near the shore, the croc will pull the animal into the water to drown it. The croc will twist or roll around over and over again with the animal clamped in its jaws until its prey is dead.

▶ **This Black Caiman is hiding in the foliage waiting for its prey to enter the water.**

By Sharon Earnest

Do crocs feed their young?

No, croc babies find their own food. Mother crocodilians do stay close to their babies, though, to protect them from enemies.

By Sharon Earnest

◄ Once the Yacare Caiman hatches, it will try to go to the water and start feeding on snails and insects. Most of the time, its mother helps it.

▼ When the croc is underwater, with only its eyes and nostrils sticking out, it can move towards its prey without being noticed.

By Terry Christopher

How does a croc use its tail for hunting?

The croc usually just glides in the water, but when it is going after its prey, its powerful tail propels it through the water silently and at a rapid speed.

Do crocs get fat?

Wild crocs do not get fat, but those that live in captivity sometimes put on too much weight.

▼ This pair of Cuban Crocodiles are being kept on a crocodile farm. Crocs on farms often get fat because of lack of exercise.

By Sharon Earnest

Do crocs get skinny?

Crocs never look really skinny, like some people do. In the winter or during changes in the environment, such as a cold spell, crocs may seem thinner, but actually they are surviving well on food they've stored in their tail.

Is it really true that crocs store food in their tail?

Yes, crocs store food as fat. This is how they can go without eating for such long periods of time. They live on the store of fat in various parts of their bodies, including their tail.

44

How long can crocs go without eating?

Babies can survive up to four months and adults have been known to go as long as two years!

By Terry Christopher

Do some crocs really eat rocks?

All crocodilians eat rocks or stones. When they can't find stones, they eat pebbles or gravel or bits of wood or other hard things. These stones are not like regular food. They stay inside the croc's stomach and help to grind up their food. Some scientists think that the stones keep a crocodilian from feeling hungry. Others think that the extra weight helps it to swim and dive better and to stay stable in the water.

▲ The croc's body uses its food so efficiently that most adult crocs eat only about 50 meals a year.

▼ Nile Crocodiles are among the most ferocious eaters of all crocs. They will often feed together as a group until the carcass of their prey is gone.

By Sharon Earnest

CROCODILIAN REPRODUCTION

◄ You can see three eggs in this Yacare Caiman nest. There are probably more underneath them.

By Sharon Earnest

▲ Crocodilians have little bumps under their jaw. These are musk glands and they show that the crocodilian is starting to mature. These glands produce a scent that attracts the opposite sex. They are more noticeable on males.

By Sharon Earnest

How do crocodilians mate? How do mother crocodilians build nests? How long does it take for the babies to hatch? Crocodilians are one of the few reptiles that take care of their babies until they are old enough to be on their own. Crocs nuzzle, chat and eat together—just like families!

How do crocs court each other?

Females raise their heads out of the water, and puff out their throats. Both sexes make bellowing and grunting noises as their interest in mating increases. During this process, females gently nuzzle or bump the males, and may even climb onto their backs.

By Dr. James Dixon, Texas A&M University

▲ If you look very closely through the trees, you can see these two American Alligators courting.

Do crocs make sounds when they mate?

Crocodilians communicate by making grunting sounds in their throats. When they bellow loudly, they sound like dogs barking. They make both of these sounds when mating, and at other times as well. The voices of the males are usually deeper than those of the females.

▼ These American Alligators are mating in the water.

How do crocodilians mate?

Mating always takes place in the water. After courting, the male and female crocodilians swim side by side until she lets him intertwine with her. The male has one reproductive organ that is inserted into the female's cloaca. The crocs' cloacas attach and mating takes place. Group matings also occur. One male will mate with several females in the group.

By Sharon Earnest

How many times a year do crocs mate?

Only once, in spring or early summer.

Do all crocodilians lay eggs?

Yes, all 26 species lay eggs, either in holes on the banks of sandbars or in nests that the females of some species build.

▶ This baby Saltwater Crocodile is emerging from its shell.

By Sharon Earnest

How large are crocodilian eggs?

The size of the eggs depends on the size of the mother. The eggs are oval-shaped and white or ivory in color.

▶ **Generally, crocodilian eggs are the size of the eggs you buy at the store.**

By Dr. James Dixon, Texas A&M University

How many eggs do crocodilians lay?

Crocodilians may lay anywhere from a dozen to 90 eggs at a time. Gharials may lay 16–61, but they usually lay about 36–37. The Saltwater Crocodile averages 50 eggs, but the range may be 25–90. The number of eggs, like their size, depends on the mother. Older females produce more eggs.

By Sharon Earnest

◀ **These American Alligator eggs are just about ready to hatch.**

How long do croc eggs take to hatch?

This varies with the species and the temperature. Scientists believe it can take anywhere from 55 to 110 days for the babies to emerge from their eggs.

By Sharon Earnest

◀ This baby American Alligator is getting ready to come out of its shell. It's making grunting noises, calling for its mother.

▼ The baby is struggling to get out of its egg.

By Sharon Earnest

▲ If you look closely, you can see the baby's feet and head sticking out of this egg.

By Sharon Earnest

▲ At last, after a long, exhausting process, this little Morelet's Crocodile comes out of its egg.

▼ Baby caimans, like all other crocs, often need help hatching. Their mothers do this by gently breaking open the egg and waiting for the baby to come out.

▲ As you see, baby crocs often take a break so they can rest up before completely leaving their shells.

Can weather affect crocodilian babies?

Yes. Since water can seep through crocodilian eggshells, too much rain can drown the babies before they are born. Many cloudy days can cause the temperature inside the eggs to drop too low for the babies to survive. And if the weather is too hot, the inside of the egg may overheat. This hardens the yolk so that the baby can't absorb it and starves to death.

▼ This Morelet's Crocodile has just broken free from its egg. Like other crocs, it will feed on the yolk sac from its egg for the first 2—14 days of its life.

51

By Sharon Earnest

▲ This croc is a few months old. Like all baby crocs, it is very curious and will eat anything it can catch.

Why is the temperature inside the nest important?

Scientists believe that the temperature inside the nest decides the sex of the alligator or crocodile. Higher temperatures, like 89–91°F (32–33°C) produce more males, while lower temperatures, such as 88°F (31°C) or lower produce more females. Temperature also affects the color and body patterns of the babies. Temperatures lower than 82°F (28°C) will kill the babies before they can hatch.

Do most baby crocs survive in the wild?

Crocodilians are at the highest risk of losing their lives in their first year. Experts have guessed that as many as 9 out of 10 die during this time! When crocodilian eggs are first laid, they are in the most danger.

By Sharon Earnest

▲ Newly hatched crocs are often the prey of birds, mammals and large fish.

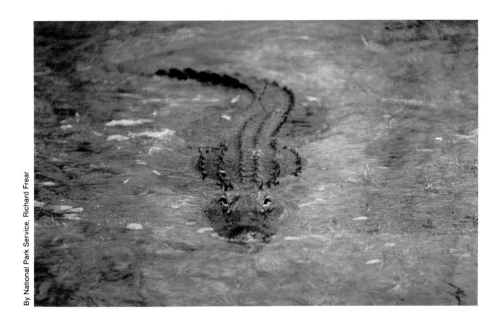

By National Park Service, Richard Frear

What are croc nests made from?

Usually leaves, forest debris and soil make up the croc's nest. They help keep the eggs warm. Many crocodilian nests are hidden away from predators along river banks.

◀ This female American Alligator, even though in the water, always remains close to her nest.

Do other animals ever share a croc nest?

Yes, sometimes, turtles lay their eggs in crocodilian nests. They take advantage of the hard work the croc has done in providing a safe place for the eggs. The baby turtles hatch and leave the nest before the crocodilians do.

▶ The Arru turtles of South America often lay their eggs in caiman nests.

By Terry Christopher

How do females protect their eggs?

Female crocs build two types of nests.

1. The mound nest is made of sand and earth combined with grasses, underwater plants and leaves. The female lays between 5 and 90 large white eggs, which she guards while they develop.

2. The hole nest is simply a hole dug into the sand or earth on the bank of a slow-moving river, in which the female deposits her eggs. Female crocodilians construct their nests so that the temperature is just right for the eggs.

By Sharon Earnest

▲ After the Yacare Caiman finishes laying her eggs, she covers them with plants to keep them warm.

▼ The Nile Crocodile is a "sand" or "hole" nester.

By Dr. James Dixon, Texas A&M University

▲ **This is a mound nest. Its average size is about 6 feet (1.8 m) in diameter and 1—3 feet (.3—.9m) high.**

By Sharon Earnest

54

Do crocodilians make good parents?

Yes. For example, the female American Alligator, like all crocodilians, gently carries her newly hatched babies to the water in her mouth, and guards them for most of the first year of their lives. She also lets them ride on her back.

Is there a special name for baby crocs?

Newborn crocs are called "neonates." As they grow older, they are called "juveniles."

How long do baby crocs take to grow up?

It depends on the species, but it takes five or six years to reach maturity. The average length of a croc when it's mature is 5–6 feet (1.5–1.8 m) long.

▶ **This may be the first photo ever taken in the wild of a Siamese Crocodile hatching. That's because there are so few of this species left.**

How fast do croc babies grow?

If the temperature and food supply are right, young crocodilians can grow very quickly. They may grow as long as 15–24 inches (38–61 cm) within a year.

By Sharon Earnest

55

SELF-DEFENSE

◄ When the territory of the American Crocodile is invaded, the croc usually opens its mouth and roars loudly, thrashing with its tail.

▼ The South American Anaconda, the largest snake in the world, preys on the caiman. Caimans are this snake's favorite food.

Depending on where the crocodiles and alligators live, raccoons, skunks, coyotes, wild pigs, monitor lizards and even rats are among the many animals that eat croc eggs. As the crocodilians grow older, they are in less danger. On dry land, lions, jaguars or even African elephants may kill them. In water, hippopotamuses may attack them. But the number-one enemy of crocs is Man.

By Terry Christopher

By Terry Christopher

▲ People hunt crocs, no matter what their size. Sometimes these creatures are killed for their skin; sometimes they are killed for no reason at all.

By Brian Parker. Tom Stack & Assoc.

By Sharon Earnest

◄ These Brown Caimans, like other crocodilians, are easy to mistake for floating logs.

How do crocs protect themselves?

Crocodilians are excellent swimmers and may flee from larger animals by taking to the water where they feel much more secure. They may spend hours almost completely underwater, waiting for the danger to pass.

Crocs are also protected by their coloring, which blends in with their surroundings. Many species change color continually. For instance, in warm parts of the day, they may become lighter in color. In cool parts of the day, such as the morning, they may look duller and are often mistaken for logs.

By Sharon Earnest

▲ The Mugger Crocodile, also known as the Indian Marsh Crocodile, often lays low in the swamps during the day to avoid confrontations with humans.

Why do crocs bury themselves in the mud?

Crocodilians submerge themselves in large mud deposits for protection against their enemies and also against other crocodilians. Nile Crocodiles are famous for doing this. Crocs also bury themselves in the mud to control their body temperature.

▶ **This Morelet's Crocodile is in the mud, hiding from danger.**

By Dr. James Dixon, Texas A&M University

By Dr. James Dixon, Texas A&M University

▲ **This young, Smooth-fronted Caiman, like many other crocodilians, can move quickly on land to escape enemies.**

Are crocodilians good runners?

Although crocodilians usually move slowly on land, they can move fast when they need to. Running speed depends on the size and type of croc, but it ranges between 3 and 11 miles (5 km–17.7 km) per hour. Compared to humans, crocs aren't very fast runners. Small crocodilians would rather hide than run.

How else does a crocodilian protect himself?

The crocodilian's powerful jaws, strong tail and heavy armor all aid the animal in protecting itself.

▲ Most crocodilians, like this Siamese Crocodile, have thick scales and large bony plates embedded in their skin. Their hides are very tough. Killing a crocodilian would exhaust even the strongest hunter.

▶ All crocodilians can inflate their bodies to larger than their normal size. By letting out air quickly, they create a deep hissing sound that scares most intruders away.

Do crocodilians fight?

Some scientists say no, that crocs defend their territories simply by opening their mouths and inflating their bodies. This takes less energy than fighting and is safer for any animal. But, if bluffing doesn't work, combat will result and can become violent. Combat between large Australian Saltwater Crocodiles involves head-ramming and tail-thrashing. This behavior can continue for more than an hour!

▼ Many crocodilians lose limbs or parts of their tail, and even die in battles over territory.

By Sharon Earnest

CROCODILIANS AND PEOPLE

◄ **Although it is a threatened species, the Spectacled Caiman is starting to make a comeback in its wild state through government protection.**

Crocodilians, like many species of reptile, are both cautious and curious. This can make them very dangerous to approach. If you meet a crocodilian in the wild, the best thing to do is turn around, walk away slowly and leave it alone. Crocs get agitated very easily. They may be bigger than you, but they are not used to human beings and they're scared of them.

How do you kow when a croc is going to attack?

A crocodilian lets you know when it is alarmed. It puffs up its body, hisses and often makes loud noises. This often leads to an attack, as the croc tries to defend itself.

▶ **Caimans protect their territory and when approached by other animals or humans, they become very defensive.**

By Sharon Earnest

Do crocodilians ever eat people?

There have been a number of documented cases in Africa, Australia and the United States of large crocodilians attacking and killing humans. A Saltwater Crocodile, Nile Crocodile or American Alligator will grab a person who is swimming, fishing or washing in its area. Or, it may attack a person who has fallen out of a boat. Sometimes a croc will attack a boat instead of the people swimming away! Croc attacks on people are extremely rare and are generally motivated by fear or hunger.

▲ Caimans, such as the Brown Caiman, sometimes wander into areas where humans swim or play, such as golf courses and swimming holes.

Do people keep crocs as pets?

Alligators and caimans were once sold as pets in large numbers all over the world. However, many died because they were not properly cared for.

▼ Crocodilians do not make good pets because they belong in the wild. It is unfair to an animal to keep it in poor living conditions, such as basements. These animals need sunlight and exercise to stay healthy.

Do people ever eat crocodilians?

Yes, for many cultures worldwide, crocodilians are a food source. In the United States, the American Alligator is often served as a delicacy in expensive restaurants. In Cajun restaurants in the southeastern United States they are listed on the menu as "alligator nuggets."

Is it true that pet owners once released crocodilians into lakes, rivers and sewers?

Yes, in the early 1970s, many baby crocodilians were sold as pets, but their owners were unable to care for them. So people released them into lakes, rivers and sewer systems in the United States and the United Kingdom. Most of these animals died of the winter cold, but some populations survive to this day. One example is the Brown Caiman, which can be found in the canal systems of Florida.

Are all crocodilians endangered?

All crocodilians are protected and 21 out of 26 species are recognized as endangered or threatened.

▲ Crocodile eggs are often stolen and sold. This photograph shows a nest that has been tampered with.

▲ Morelet's Crocodiles are considered an endangered species.

▶ Orinoco Crocodiles are extremely rare because their habitat has been destroyed.

What is being done to help crocodilians survive?

Many alligator and crocodile farms are breeding rare crocodilians so that they may be returned to the wild. There are laws such as the Cites treaty that make it illegal to touch, harm, capture or kill crocs, protecting them from poachers. Cites stands for Convention on International Trade in Endangered Species, and more than 80 nations observe it.

What are poachers?

Poachers are people who hunt animals illegally for sport or profit. They kill animals for their skins or other body parts. They also take animals alive and sell them to animal dealers and collectors. Poaching is a crime. If caught, most poachers go to jail.

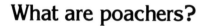
By Sharon Earnest

By Sharon Earnest

▲ All the crocodilian species in the world today are capable of making a comeback through present conservation efforts.

◄ This African Dwarf Crocodile is being kept at an alligator farm for breeding. If it wasn't for crocodile farms and the work they do, most crocodilian species would be extinct today.

By National Park Service, Richard Frear

What is a crocodile farm?

It's a place where crocs are raised and protected from people who might hurt them. The farm consists of many acres of land with canals and ponds.

How can I help?

Some people donate time or money to such organizations as the World Wildlife Fund that help protect animals all over the world.

▲ Due to conservation techniques in Florida, the American Alligator was saved from extinction and is now flourishing.

By Sharon Earnest

◄ This Philippine Crocodile once lived in the Philippines in large numbers. Now only about 100 exist in the wild.

67

If I wanted to work with crocodilians, what would I need to study?

You would study herpetology and learn all about crocodilians, snakes, lizards, turtles and amphibians. If you want to talk to herpetologists, some good places to meet them are museums, zoos and universities.

Where can I go to see crocodilians?

Start with your local conservation center. Some of them have many species of reptile. One of the best places to see many different species is a crocodile ranch. These government-supported non-profit companies, like croc farms, breed the animals so that they can later be released in the wild.

▼ There are only a few institutions around the world that get the opportunity to work with and breed Indian gharials.

By Doug Perrine, Innerspace Visions

▲ Not many photographers are willing to get into the water with alligators! This is a rare shot of an American Alligator underwater.

By Sharon Earnest

68

By Terry Christopher

How do crocs affect the food chain?

Crocs' wastes provide important nutrients for smaller animals in the food chain, such as fish and frogs. Scientists have discovered that the number of fish in some areas decreases when the number of crocs decrease.

▲ Crocodiles and alligators play an important role in today's environment and food chain.

69

GREAT CROCS

What is a family and what is a species of crocodilian?

A family is a group of crocodilians with similar features. A species is a specific kind of croc.

For example, one croc family is *crocodylinae*. A species of crocodylinae is an American Crocodile.

Another croc family is *alligatorinae*. A species of alligatorinae is an American Alligator.

A third croc family is *gavialinae*. The only species of gavialinae is the gharial.

By Sharon Earnest

▲ Very few people have ever seen a baby American Crocodile. Crocs of this species hide in the wild until they mature.

How are crocodilians named?

Scientists called taxonomists help to identify animals and name them. The names sometimes tell what they look like, where they live, or myths about them. Crocs have common names that are easy to remember but can change from country to country. Crocs also have scientific names. For example, one species of croc has the common name of Saltwater Crocodile and in Australia it is called a "Salty." Its scientific name is *Crocodylus porosus*, and that is the same all around the world.

By Terry Christopher

By Terry Christopher

▲ The American Alligator was named for the place it lives in. It is one of only two alligator species.

◄ These baby Philippine Crocodiles are just a day old. This species can be found only in the freshwater swamps, lakes and rivers of the Philippine islands of Mindero, Negros, Mindanao and Samar.

▼ American Alligators have a nickname in Florida. They're called "gators."

By National Park Service, Cecil W. Stoughton

By Sharon Earnest

▲ The Mugger Crocodile has the broadest head of any croc.

What crocodile has the strangest name?

The Mugger Crocodile got its name because it has been known to snatch fish right out of fishermen's nets.

What is the largest crocodile in the world?

It is probably the awesome Saltwater Crocodile, the species that appeared in the movie *Crocodile Dundee*. Many grow to the length of 23 feet (7m). Some 30-foot (9m) specimens have been reported in Australia.

▼ Saltwater Crocodiles live in many places around the world, including eastern India, Southeast Asia and Australia.

By Sharon Earnest

▲ Nile Crocodiles of tropical Africa are also some of the largest in the world—18 feet (5.5m)—but they are hunted so much that few grow to the maximum length.

What are the smallest crocs in the world?

The African Dwarf Crocodile is one of the smallest species. Even smaller may be the Cuvier's Dwarf Caiman. Males may grow to 5 feet (1.5m), females about 4 feet (1.2m).

▼ According to scientists, many species of Dwarf Caiman are especially afraid of humans and even adults will shy away when encountered.

By Sharon Earnest

▲ Baby African Dwarf Crocodiles are seldom photographed, because they are so hard to find in the wild.

By Sharon Earnest

What is the strangest-looking crocodilian?

Perhaps the Indian Gharial is the strangest. It has heavy armor and a narrow snout that is longer than any other croc's—plus about 100 very sharp, pointed teeth.

▲ Gharials are poor walkers. Their back legs aren't as strong as other crocs' and their toes have more webbing.

▶ Conservationists are collecting Indian Gharial eggs for use in repopulation programs.

By Sharon Earnest

▲ The Australian Freshwater Crocodile is also known as the Johnston's Crocodile. It is extremely endangered.

What are the rarest crocodiles?

Many species of croc are very rare and seldom seen, such as the Philippine Crocodile and the Australian Freshwater Crocodile, whose habitats have been built upon by humans.

▶ Morelet's Crocodile babies are seldom seen. It is believed that they like to feed on insects and snails near the water's edge.

By R. Reed

▲ The endangered Cuban Crocodile is now protected by the Cuban government.

By Sharon Earnest

By Sharon Earnest

▲ Siamese Crocodiles are also very rare. Only about 200 exist in the world today.

What is the rarest alligator?

Of the two species of alligators, the Chinese Alligator is more endangered. Only 500 are known to survive in the wild today.

By Terry Christopher

▲ The Chinese Alligator digs or burrows for shelter, which is very unusual for a crocodilian.

Are gharials endangered?

Yes; according to scientists, there are only 120 true gharials left in the wild.

What is the rarest caiman?

Probably the Cuvier's Dwarf Caiman is the rarest. It lives in parts of the Amazon River Basin. It prefers rocky places that are hard to reach for the people who study it.

▼ Studies of the contents of the stomach of the Cuvier's Dwarf Caiman suggest that these caimans sometimes eat their young.

What is the largest caiman?

Adult Black Caimans can measure 20 feet (6m) or more. They live in South America, where they are also the largest predators.

▶ Although the Black Caiman is the largest species of caiman, the Brown Caiman runs a close second, averaging 6–8 feet (1.8–2.5m) in length.

▼ Black Caimans are endangered because of poaching and the loss of their habitat.

By Sharon Earnest

By Sharon Earnest

79

Acknowledgments

We would like to thank the following people for their help and support on this project: Dr. James Dixon and the staff at Texas A & M University, Rick Reed from the Fort Worth Zoo and Sharon and Ken Earnest, Terry Christopher, Jeff Martin, and thanks to the staffs at Reptile Gardens in South Dakota and at the National Park Service.

We would like to thank the following families and friends: Mike, Ryan, Carly and Matthew Stone, Esther Clover, Terrell and Scott Fortner, Diane and Royce Smith, Art and Elva Stone, Linda and Sarah Stone, Shaun and Linda Smith, Ron Smith, Pat and Renée Cooper, John and Sandy Johnson and Mike Cooper. Also thanks to Sherrie Stoops, Alesha Stoops and Corrine Konz.

Also a special thanks to Mrs. Whigham's 1992–1993 second grade class at Kyrene Monte Vista school in Phoenix for wanting answers to their questions about crocs.

Index